SECRET MESSAGES

a collection of puzzles using codes and ciphers

JEFF HAWTIN

CODE WORDS

cipher: a secret rule for changing individual letters of an ordinary plaintext message into a cryptogram or secret message.

cipher alphabet: a set of symbols, numbers or letters used to represent the 26 letters of the alphabet.

code: a rule for replacing letters, words or groups of words with letters, signs or symbols.

codebreaker: the common word used in ordinary speech for a cryptanalyst.

cryptanalyst: someone who tries to break or decipher cryptograms without having the key.

cryptogram: a message in which the original words are hidden according to a cipher or code.

cryptographer: someone who studies the art of secret writing and invents new codes and ciphers.

cryptography: the art of secret writing.

decipher: to turn a cryptogram or secret message back into an ordinary plaintext message.

encipher: to turn an ordinary plaintext message into a cryptogram or secret message.

null: a meaningless letter, number or sign used in a cryptogram or secret message.

plaintext: any message written in its original sensible language.

substitution cipher: a cipher which replaces all the letters of an original plaintext message with letters, signs or numbers.

transposition cipher: a cipher which keeps all the letters of the original plaintext message unchanged but moves them out of their correct order.

© 2001:   Jeff Hawtin
© 1990:   First Edition
I.S.B.N: 0 906212 78 2
Design: Susan Apling
Printing: Fuller-Davies Ltd., Ipswich

CE

Tarquin Publications
Stradbroke
Diss
Norfolk IP21 5JP
England

CODES and CIPHERS

A message written in ordinary English is said to be in *plaintext*. If the message contains information which is supposed to be secret then it has to be kept in a safe place and restricted only to those who have the right security clearance. Anyone who looks at it can see immediately what it says. However, once it is *enciphered* and becomes a *cryptogram*, it does not matter who sees it. It becomes an apparently meaningless string of letters or symbols. Such cryptograms can be sent by post, by radio, by telephone or indeed written on banners and strung across the street. Unless the key is known, it cannot be read.

That at least is the theory. Because for just as long as people have tried to hide their secret messages as cryptograms, others have tried to read the messages by breaking or *deciphering* the codes and ciphers. Such people were called *cryptanalysts* and they have always been important assistants to kings, generals and diplomats. In such fields as trade, politics and warfare it is very valuable indeed to know the plans of a rival, an opponent or an enemy in advance. Once leaders realised that their messages could be read by an opponent they started to employ *cryptographers* to devise new or better ciphers. Often a cryptographer and a cryptanalyst was one and the same person. No-one was better placed to design a new cipher than someone who knew how to break them. This competition to discover other people's secrets and to hide their own has existed since man first learned to write and no doubt will continue for as long as there are humans on our planet.

In this book there are 16 different ciphers which give a good idea of some of the methods used by cryptographers over the years. Some hardly hide the message at all, but some would be very difficult for any cryptanalyst to break quickly. This point about the time needed to break a cipher is a very important one because most secrets only need to be kept secret for a limited period. For instance, it does not matter if an enemy can read the plans for a battle three weeks after the battle has taken place. If that cipher takes that long to break, then it is a good cipher for its purpose.

Apart from messages to encipher and decipher this book contains four cut-out cryptographic devices. They make it easier to avoid errors and are interesting in themselves, but they also serve a more serious purpose. They illustrate the first steps towards machines which can encipher and decipher automatically and so reduce the risk of copying errors. The earliest machines were developed from typewriters and telegraph machines and were so arranged that when a plaintext letter was typed in, the machine automatically produced the cipher letter. Nowadays this task has been taken over by computers, indeed the very first computers were developed for cryptanalysis purposes. Most enciphering and deciphering is now done automatically and at high speed by electronic computers. The programs grow ever more sophisticated, but the principle remains the same as the ciphers in this book. The plaintext has to be converted into a cryptogram by means of a *transposition* or a *substitution* or a combination of both.

On reading this book you may be surprised to see the word *cipher* used so much more than the word *code*. Both codes and ciphers are used for secret messages and in common speech people often talk of cryptanalysts as *codebreakers*. The difference is really one of degree. If a plaintext is changed into a cryptogram letter by letter then the correct word to use is cipher. A code usually converts complete words or groups of words into cryptograms. For instance "36" might mean "meet me at the railway station at noon". Codes may be short and convenient but they are very limited because both people have to agree exactly what they mean and both need a codebook which could be acquired by an opponent or captured by an enemy. Most secret messages are sent using ciphers and codes are mostly used for making information public and easy to handle. The telephone dialling codes and postal codes are good examples of non-secret codes set up for easy public use. The semaphore code is an example of a letter by letter public code used in the past for communicating from ship to ship. In this book it is used to pass on a further secret message.

READY TO START

RANDOM BREAK CIPHERS

In this cipher, neither the letters of the plaintext nor their order is changed, but the eye is deliberately misled by introducing unexpected breaks in the words. This may well be enough to confuse someone who does not know what to look for. Furthermore it has the advantage of being very easy to use in both enciphering and deciphering messages.

_____Examples_____

A

plaintext ➡ THE CAR IS PARKED ON QUEEN STREET

cryptogram ➡ TH ECA RISP ARK EDONQ UEE NST REET

B

plaintext ➡ WE LEFT OUR CAR AT HOME

cryptogram ➡ WEL EF TOURC ARATH OME

PUZZLES

___Messages to Encipher___

1. WAIT FOR THE WEATHER TO CLEAR
2. WRITE DOWN THEIR ADDRESS FOR ME
3. THEY WILL BE ABLE TO VISIT TODAY

___Messages to Decipher___

4. WH YWA ST HECRA BSE NTTO PRIS ON
5. BECA USEH EKEP TPINC HIN GTHI NGS
6. WHI CHTOO THP AS TEDO SHA RKSU SE
7. TH EYUS EAQU AFLES HOFCO U RSE
8. WHYD IDT HEFIS HBLU SH
9. BECA USEI TSA WTH EOCE ANSBO TTOM

ZIGZAG CIPHERS

To write a message in a zigzag cipher, the plaintext letters remain unchanged but they are mixed by the simple process of writing them above and below one or more horizontal lines.

The letters which occur on each line are written out in their groups and the groups themselves are separated by spaces or dots.

_____Examples_____

A

plaintext ➡ I CAN WRITE A ZIGZAG CIPHER

```
  I   A W I   E Z G A C P   E
_____
    C N   R T A   I Z G I H R
```

cryptogram ➡ IAWIEZGACPE.CNRTAIZGIHR

B

plaintext ➡ CAN YOU WRITE A ZIGZAG CIPHER

```
  C   O     I     Z     A     P
_____
    A Y U R T A I Z G I H R
_____
    N   W   E   G   C   E
```

cryptogram ➡ COIZAP.AYURTAIZGIHR .NWEGCE

PUZZLES

___Messages to Encipher___

1. I RELAX AT THE WEEKEND
   (as example A)
2. THIS CIPHER IS EASY TO USE
   (as example B)
3. WE ENJOY LISTENING TO MUSIC
   (as examples A and B)

___Messages to Decipher___

4. WIEORETRCERY.RTYULTESLAL
5. MTPS.AEHSAEBG.KECI
6. WRSEDLADAEUL.OKTAIYNCRFLY
7. DZHOOZ.OTAWEYUHUDI.NGNSLG

WHAT IS THE DIFFERENCE BETWEEN A SCRATCHING DOG AND A RUNNING FOX?

8. OUFSTTFST.NHNSLAADHOHRLEHNS.ETENEEEU

SQUARE CIPHERS

In this cipher the plaintext letters remain unchanged but they are *transposed* by writing them as rows into the grid square. The cryptogram is simply a list of the letters in each column, separated by spaces. To decipher secret messages of this type, you have to reverse the process. Write them vertically into the square, but read them horizontally.

_____Examples_____

A   plaintext ➡ COME AT TWO

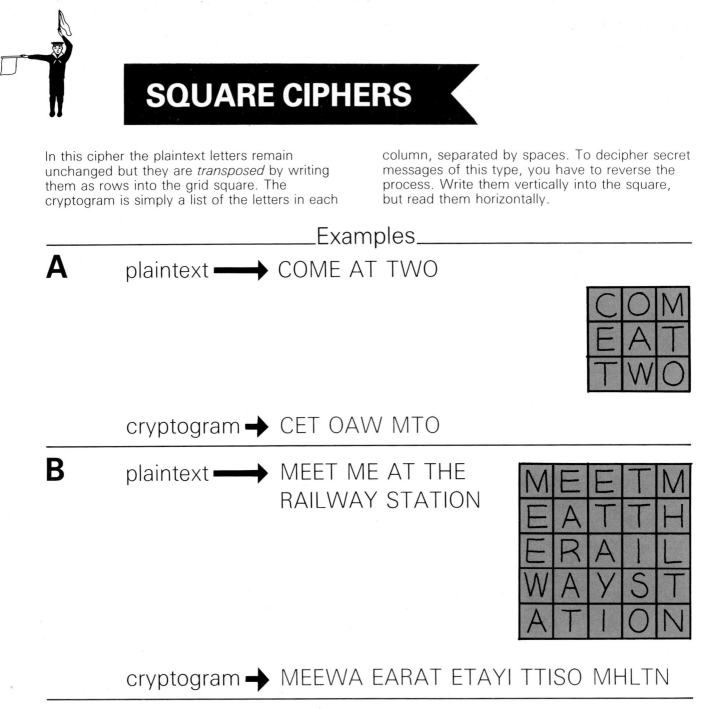

cryptogram ➡ CET OAW MTO

B   plaintext ➡ MEET ME AT THE RAILWAY STATION

cryptogram ➡ MEEWA EARAT ETAYI TTISO MHLTN

8

PUZZLES

___Messages to Encipher___

1. MAKE A GRID
2. PUT IN ALL THE WORDS
3. WRITE EACH COLUMN FROM THE TOP
4. HERE IS OUR NEW SECRET MESSAGE

___Messages to Decipher___

5. OMU NIT ENE
6. FRU OHR UOS
7. SNSW EDIE VANE EYAK
8. FTEKH IWKEY FOSEE TWMAA YEACR

WHAT IS THE DIFFERENCE BETWEEN A PILOT AND A CARPENTER?

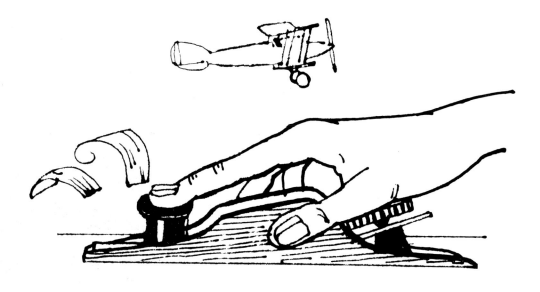

9. ORNSPB NDEELO ESSCAA BPTONR OLHNED AAEDSS

RECTANGLE CIPHERS

This cipher is a simple variation on the rows and columns idea of the square cipher. The letters are written into a rectangular grid whose size is determined by the number of letters in the message. If the receiver knows that it is a rectangle cipher, then the grouping of the letters in the cryptogram indicates what shape the rectangle is.

Examples

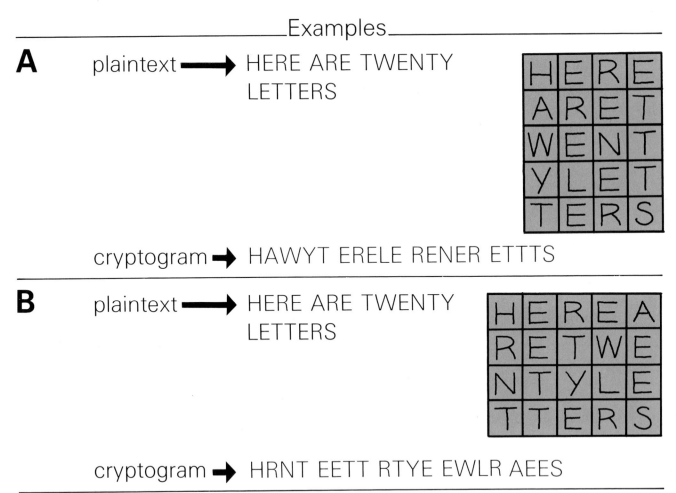

A   plaintext ➡ HERE ARE TWENTY LETTERS

cryptogram ➡ HAWYT ERELE RENER ETTTS

B   plaintext ➡ HERE ARE TWENTY LETTERS

cryptogram ➡ HRNT EETT RTYE EWLR AEES

PUZZLES

___Messages to Encipher___

Make cryptograms using 5 or 6 columns

1. I AM IN BIG TROUBLE
2. GO QUICKLY TO AMERICA
3. GET ME A FORGED PASSPORT
4. HERE IT IS. GOOD LUCK IN AMERICA

___Messages to Decipher___

5. JBM AEB CNL KIE
6. PPN EUG ADH SDO EIT
7. BAAH AACE ABKE BLSP
8. OTBKMH NWULYO EOCESE
9. SIA IMP MOI PNE LMM EEA STN

CROSSWORD

10 Find a country to complete the crossword.

a) MDGSA AAACR
b) GEA RNN ELD
c) ATL URI SAA
d) SA RN IK LA
e) MRI AIU UTS
f) NGN EUE WIA
g) ????? ???????

RECTANGLES and NULLS

These puzzles introduce the idea of *nulls* or meaningless letters which help both to hide the message and to make it fit into a rectangle of a convenient size. In these examples less frequently used letters like X, Y, Z were chosen as nulls as it is less confusing for the recipient of the cryptogram. However in theory any letter can be chosen as long as both the sender and the recipient knows what it is.

_____Examples_____

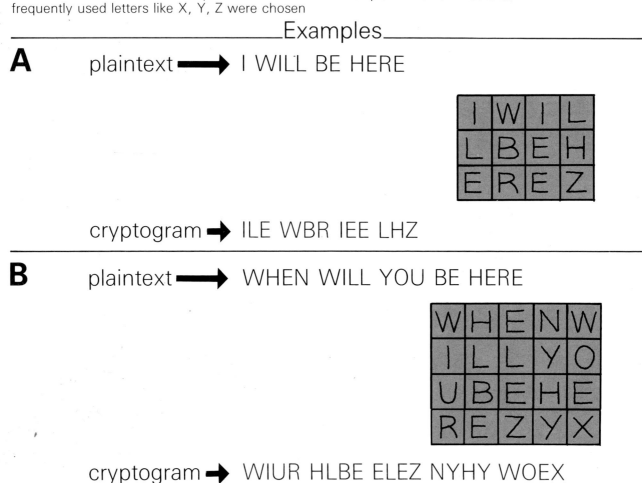

A   plaintext ➡ I WILL BE HERE

I	W	I	L
L	B	E	H
E	R	E	Z

cryptogram ➡ ILE WBR IEE LHZ

B   plaintext ➡ WHEN WILL YOU BE HERE

W	H	E	N	W
I	L	L	Y	O
U	B	E	H	E
R	E	Z	Y	X

cryptogram ➡ WIUR HLBE ELEZ NYHY WOEX

___Messages to Encipher___

Make cryptograms using 5 columns
Use Q for each null

1. TEAR UP THE PAPER

2. USE THE SPECIAL CIPHER

3. READ THIS LETTER CAREFULLY

4. PASS ON THE MESSAGE QUICKLY

5. KEEP THE NEW INFORMATION SECRET

6. DO YOU STILL REMEMBER THE
   INSTRUCTIONS

___Messages to Decipher___

7. Which famous detective was caught up in
   the missing pencil case?
   IHLO TEEZ WRBY ACIX SURW

8. Which company launches chocolate rockets?
   IRHSOR TIAPFS ITEACE SIRCOY BSOEUZ

9. How do bees get to work when it is too
   windy to fly?
   TATLNZ HVRBIE EEAYBS YTVOUY HOEMZZ

10. What do you call a dinosaur that wears
    specs?
    IAAUKU TLDTHR ILOHEU SEYISS CDONAX

WHICH ANIMAL LIVES IN TREES AND LIKES TO DRINK COKE?

11. IAAB TLCE ILOA SELR CDAX

RECTANGLES and KEYNUMBERS

This cipher introduces the idea of a *keynumber* which is used to rearrange the columns of the rectangle and to make it harder for someone who does not know the keynumber to decipher the cryptogram. Anyone who does know the keynumber, labels the grid with it and then enters the letter groups of the enciphered message into the columns in numerical order. The plaintext can then be read horizontally in the normal way. Keynumbers can be changed each day or according to some predetermined pattern known to both the sender and the receiver.

_____Examples_____

A   plaintext ➡ THE TAJ MAHAL IS IN INDIA

   keynumber ➡ 51324

   cryptogram ➡ HMIN THII EASD AANA TJLI

B   plaintext ➡ TRAFALGAR SQUARE IS IN LONDON

   keynumber ➡ 35214

   cryptogram ➡ FRRNO AAAID TLQIO ASELN RGUSN

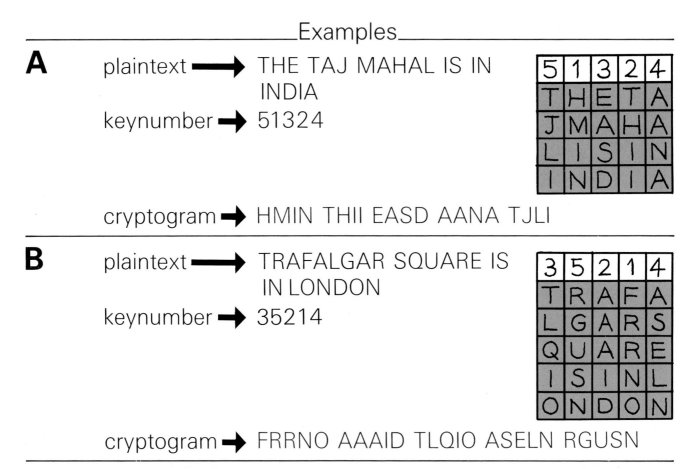

PUZZLES

___Messages to Encipher_____Messages to Decipher___

Use Z for each null

1. WILL SEND GOLD COINS
   (keynumber 32514)

2. MAKE CONTACT AS SOON AS POSSIBLE
   (keynumber 54321)

3. WE PLAN TO TRAVEL ON THE ORIENT
   EXPRESS
   (keynumber 42351)

4. What is the difference between an optician
   and a bank manager?
   HENEHS CSAECE EKSNSU NCEOEQ
   OEYDYE
   (keynumber 54321)

5. What is the difference between a group of
   stockbrokers|and convicts?
   GSSSTHCX EPSEOSSS REHTHAEX
   NULREREL OOLAHERL
   (keynumber 54213)

CROSSWORD

6. Find the town to complete the crossword

a) AS CE ME NT HR (keynumber 31425)

b) CR GE OT UE LS (keynumber 25341)

c) BE RN EE AD (keynumber 4132)

d) SL IN TI RG (keynumber 1324)

e) DBG IUH ENR (keynumber 312)

f) OS HR LT CE CE (keynumber 51342)

g) ?????????????

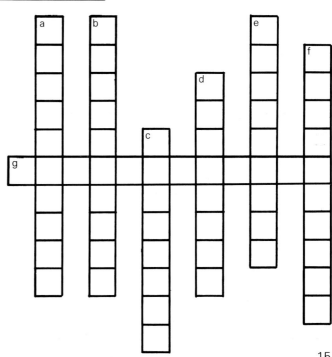

GRILLE CIPHERS

This type of cipher was first used by the Italian Jerolamo Cardano (1501-1576). The encipherer and the decipherer each has a grille, which is a piece of card with a series of windows cut into it. The two grilles are identical. To make the cipher, the grille is placed over a square grid and the plaintext is entered through the windows. All the remaining blank squares are then filled with a random mixture of other letters which act as nulls. The possessor of the correct grille can read the message with ease, provided that he or she knows which way the grille fits over the cryptogram. However, a cryptanalyst who does not know what kind of cipher it is can waste a lot of time trying to decipher the nulls.

Example
---

plaintext ➡ YOU RING HER

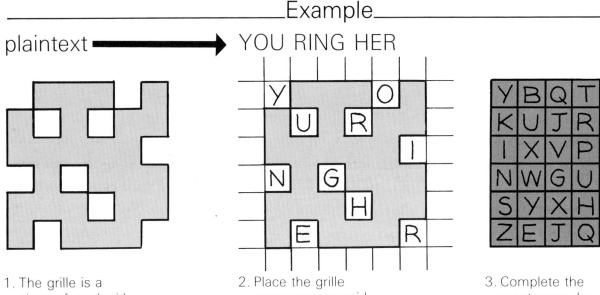

1. The grille is a piece of card with windows cut in it.

2. Place the grille over a square grid and then write the message on the squares that show.

3. Complete the cryptogram by filling in the blank squares with nulls.

cryptogram ➡ YBQTOZ KUJRLH IXVPFI NWGUDA SYXHLK ZEJQCR

CARDANO'S GRILLE

CARDANO'S GRILLE

MAKING THE CARD INSTRUMENTS

TYPE OF GLUE
To get the best results you need a glue which sets quickly but not instantly and which does not leave dirty marks. We particularly recommend UHU or a similar petroleum based glue like BOSTIC CLEAR. A white latex adhesive like COPYDEX also gives good results.

SCORING
Scoring is very important if you are to make accurate models. It makes the paper fold cleanly and accurately along the line you want. Use a ball point pen which has run out of ink and rule firmly along the fold lines. Experienced model makers may use a craft knife, but it needs care not to cut right through the paper.

GENERAL INSTRUCTIONS
1. Cut out the four pages 17, 27, 33, 39 from the book along the cut line.
2. Score along the lines marked ▶━━━◀ or (⌒) or ▶ ─ ─ ─◀
3. Cut out all of the pieces precisely including any windows or central holes.
4. Fold along each of the fold lines into either a ◿ hill ◤ fold or a ◸ valley ◹ fold

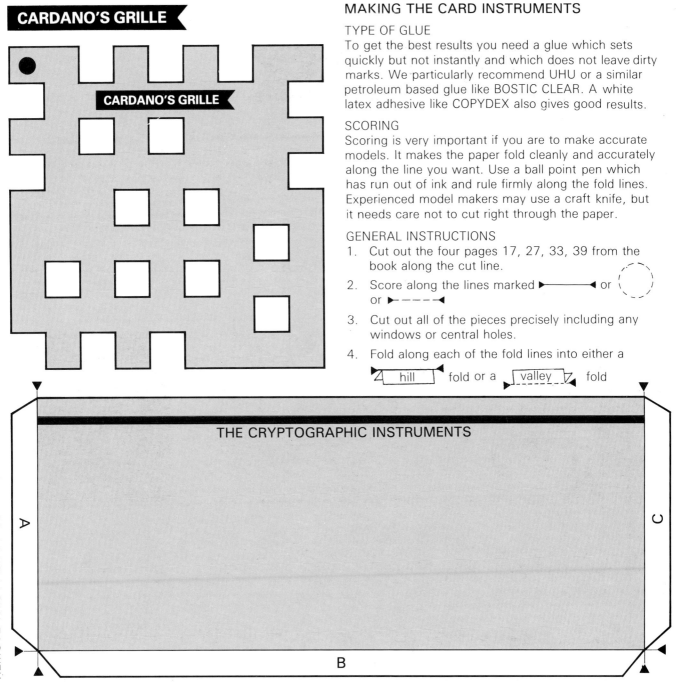

THE CRYPTOGRAPHIC INSTRUMENTS

A

C

B

VIGENERE SLIDE (page 27)

Follow the general instructions overleaf until you have the three pieces which make up the Vigenère Slide.

5. Strengthen the main part by glueing flaps A, B, C, D.

6. Make up the slide in its correct position using flaps E, F, G, H. Make certain that it is the right way up.

7. Slide it gently up and down to make sure that it moves freely and that all 26 cipher alphabets can be seen in the slot.

ALPHABET DISC (page 39)

Follow the general instructions overleaf until you have the five pieces which make up the Alphabet Disc.

5. Glue the two flaps A together and press firmly.

6. Fold teeth B upwards, pass them through pieces 2 and 3 and then glue them to piece 3.

7. Check that the disc turns freely as the glue dries.

8. Glue piece 4 to the front and piece 5 to the back using letters C and D.

9. Make sure that the disc still turns freely.

STORAGE ENVELOPE

Glue this envelope inside the back cover.

Messages to Decipher

Use Cardano's Grille to decipher these messages. There are two in each cryptogram.

 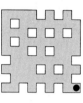  

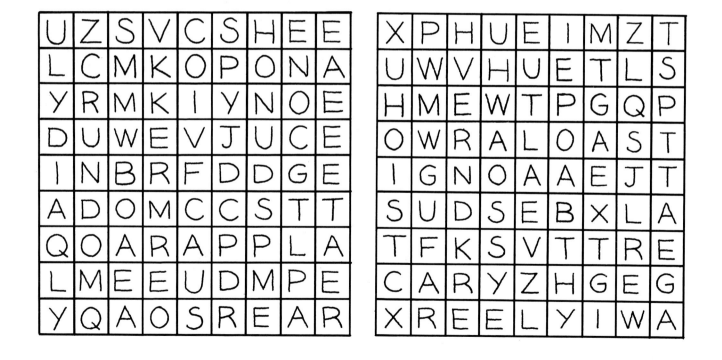

U	Z	S	V	C	S	H	E	E
L	C	M	K	O	P	O	N	A
Y	R	M	K	I	Y	N	O	E
D	U	W	E	V	J	U	C	E
I	N	B	R	F	D	D	G	E
A	D	O	M	C	C	S	T	T
Q	O	A	R	A	P	P	L	A
L	M	E	E	U	D	M	P	E
Y	Q	A	O	S	R	E	A	R

X	P	H	U	E	I	M	Z	T
U	W	V	H	U	E	T	L	S
H	M	E	W	T	P	G	Q	P
O	W	R	A	L	O	A	S	T
I	G	N	O	A	A	E	J	T
S	U	D	S	E	B	X	L	A
T	F	K	S	V	T	T	R	E
C	A	R	Y	Z	H	G	E	G
X	R	E	E	L	Y	I	W	A

OPEN LETTER CIPHERS

A good cipher will successfully hide the contents of a secret message from anyone who intercepts it, but it may not conceal the fact that a secret message is being sent. Sometimes it is most important to avoid the slightest suspicion. Spies with access to modern equipment can send a microdot. This is a photograph of the message reduced to the size of a full stop and it can be sent disguised as a real full stop in a letter. However, without such sophisticated equipment it is still possible to conceal a message in an open letter. In the example below, the first and then the last letters in each sentence have been used to make the plaintext message. It needs skill to write such a letter so that it sounds natural, but that in itself is an interesting task.

_____Example_____

plaintext ➡ YOUR HOUSE TWO O'CLOCK

cryptogram ➡

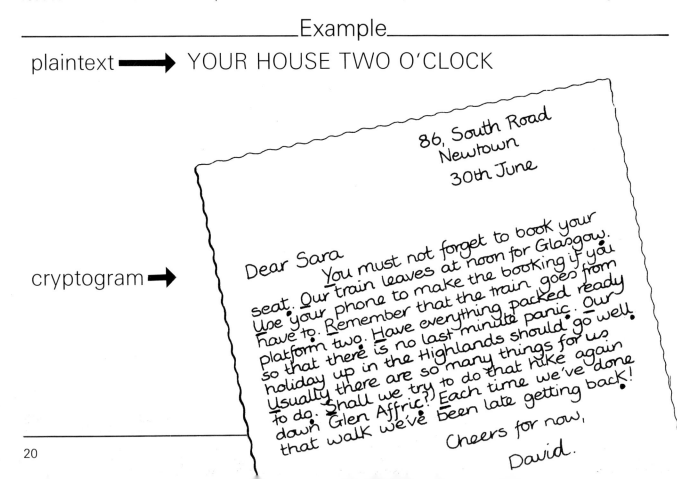

86, South Road
Newtown
30th June

Dear Sara
You must not forget to book your seat. Our train leaves at noon for Glasgow. Use your phone to make the booking if you have to. Remember that the train goes from platform two. Have everything packed ready so that there is no last minute panic. Our holiday up in the Highlands should go well. Usually there are so many things for us to do. Shall we try to do that hike again down Glen Affric? Each time we've done that walk we've been late getting back!
Cheers for now,
David.

Messages to Decipher

Two of these letters hide messages in the first and last letters of each sentence. One uses just the first word in each sentence.

Dear Sue

Five days from now and we'll be on the beach. I have been told that our hotel is very nice. No-one can stay there unless they book. Do you think we'll meet any interesting people? The time can't go quickly enough for me to get on this holiday!

See you soon
Joan

Hi Gerald!

Rovers are playing at home in the cup tie. Everyone here is hoping that they will win. All the regular supporters are certain that they will do. Drive over on Saturday and we'll make a day of it. Try to get over because I already have two tickets for the terrace. Hope it's a good game because those tickets cost me twenty pounds.

Cheerio,
Ivor.

Dear John

Book the seats for us as soon as possible. A flight leaves Heathrow for Madrid on Sunday afternoon. Taxi fares are expensive here so we'll use my car and leave it at the airport. For goodness sake don't forget your camera this time! The passports and traveller's cheques are all together in my brief case. Station yourself near the information desk and I'll be there at noon.

Be seeing you,
Steve.

Write a letter to send this message about a future meeting place.

RED ROSE CAFE
FRIDAY

21

PIG PEN CIPHER

This cipher converts plaintext letters into a pattern of lines and dots which it is hard for other people to read. A similar pattern was used widely by the freemasons during the sixteenth century. All you have to do is to draw the shapes made by the lines and dots which surround the alphabet in the diagram below.

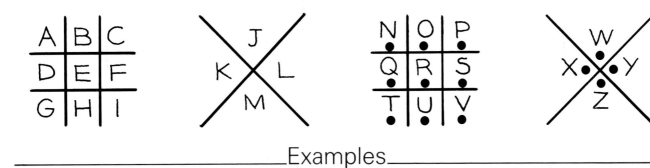

─────────────────────────Examples───────────────────────────

A   plaintext ➡ LINES AND DOTS

       cryptogram ➡ <⌐⌐⌐Oᘓ ⌐⌐⌐ ⌐ᗯ.⌐ᘓ

B   plaintext ➡ CIRCLE OR SQUARE

       cryptogram ➡ ⌐⌐⊡⌐<⊡ ᗯ⊡ ᘓⴲᐧᴎ⌐⊡⊡

PUZZLES

___Messages to Encipher___

1. THIS CIPHER IS THE PIG PEN
2. SO PLEASE USE SIMPLE SIGNS
3. REPLACE YOUR PLAINTEXT LETTERS
4. BY DRAWING DOTS AND LINES

___Messages to Decipher___

5. What do you get if you cross ⅃ ⌐ᗺ∀ ∀⌐⊐⊓ ⅃ ⊓◻⅃

6. What do you get if you cross ⅃ ⅂⊓ᗺ⋿⊓ ∀⌐⊐⊓ ⅃ ᒪᗺ<⌐⌐◻∧⅃⅃

7. What do you get if you cross ⅃ ⌐⅃⊐⊓ ∀⌐⊐⊓ ⅃ <◻∧ᗺ⅃

WHAT DO YOU GET IF YOU CROSS A SHEEPDOG WITH A JELLY?

8. ⌐⊓◻ ᒪᗺ<<⌐◻∨ᗺᗺᗺ<◻⌐

23

POLYBIUS SQUARE

This is a *substitution* cipher which converts each letter of the alphabet into a two-digit number using only the digits 1 to 5. It takes its name from its inventor, the Greek writer Polybius who lived from about 200BC to 118BC. The letters I and J have been squeezed into one square so that the English alphabet of 26 letters can be fitted in to the square grid. It would have been equally sensible for other letters such as V and W or X and Y to share a square and to achieve the same result in a different way.

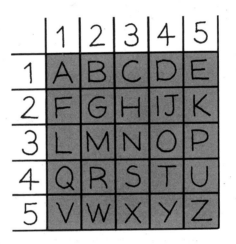

	1	2	3	4	5
1	A	B	C	D	E
2	F	G	H	IJ	K
3	L	M	N	O	P
4	Q	R	S	T	U
5	V	W	X	Y	Z

Examples

A   plaintext ➡ GOOD LUCK

cryptogram ➡ 22.34.34.14. 31.45.13.25.

B   plaintext ➡ HAPPY NEW YEAR

cryptogram ➡ 23.11.35.35.54. 33.15.52. 54.15.11.42.

___Messages to Encipher___

1. THE ANCIENT GREEK WRITER POLYBIUS
2. WROTE WORDS IN WAYS WHICH WERE DEVIOUS

___Messages to Decipher___

3. 45.43.24.33.22. 33.45.32.12.15.42.43.
   21.34.42. 31.15.44.44.15.42.43.

4. 22.42.15.11.44. 35.45.55.55.31.15.43.
   23.15.
   43.15.44. 45.43.

5. 24.33. 11. 13.24.35.23.15.42.
   32.34.42.15.
   43.15.13.42.15.44. 44.23.11.33.
   35.42.15.51.24.34.45.43.

CROSSWORD

6. Find the country to complete the crossword
   a) 43.52.15.14.15.33.
   b) 35.34.42.44.45.22.11.31.
   c) 22.42.15.15.13.15.
   d) 33.15.44.23.15.42.31.11.33.14.43.
   e) 14.15.33.32.11.42.25.
   f) ???????????

25

CAESAR'S ALPHABETS

This cipher is known as Caesar's alphabet because Julius Caesar (100BC – 44BC) used it to send letters to his friends. Each plaintext letter was replaced by a cipher letter which was three places further on in the alphabet. Because plaintext A became cipher D it was known as Caesar's D alphabet. Although Caesar used the D alphabet exclusively, there are 26 possible alphabets of this type and they are all known as Caesar's alphabets. They are classified by the letter that plaintext A becomes. The complete table of all 26 alphabets is called a Vigenère Table after Blaise de Vigenère, a Frenchman born in 1523.

Ciphers which use Caesar's alphabets are made easier to encipher and decipher by using the mechanical assistance of the card instruments, the VIGENERE SLIDE or the ALPHABET DISC.

_____Examples_____

A   plaintext ➡ CAESAR INVENTED THIS CIPHER

Encipher using Caesar's E Alphabet using the VIGENERE SLIDE

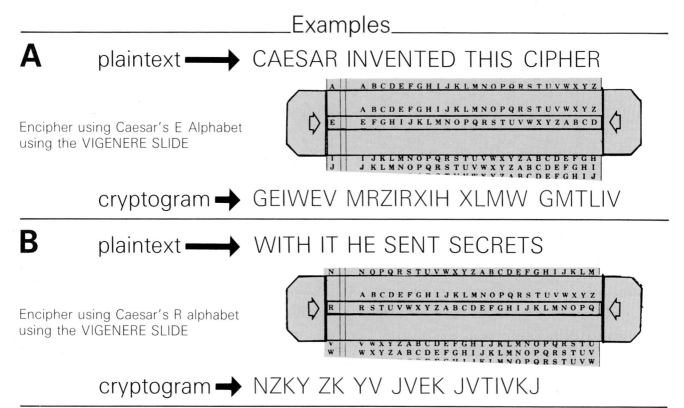

cryptogram ➡ GEIWEV MRZIRXIH XLMW GMTLIV

B   plaintext ➡ WITH IT HE SENT SECRETS

Encipher using Caesar's R alphabet using the VIGENERE SLIDE

cryptogram ➡ NZKY ZK YV JVEK JVTIVKJ

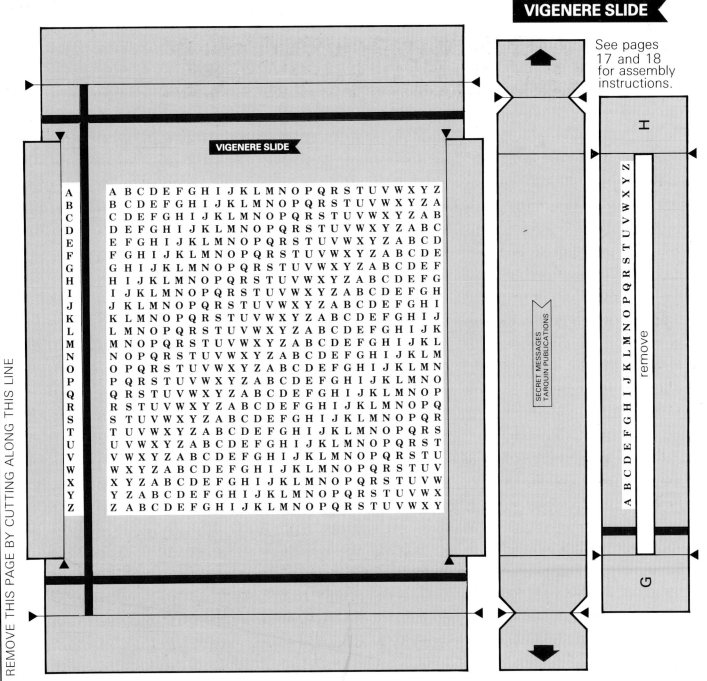

no glue

F

C

G

A

B

H

E

D

no glue

___Messages to Encipher___

1. LATIN IS A LANGUAGE (E Alphabet)

2. AS DEAD AS DEAD CAN BE (H Alphabet)

3. IT KILLED THE MIGHTY ROMANS (M Alphabet)

4. AND NOW ITS KILLING ME (Q Alphabet)

5. ITS A PITY THAT OLD GEEZER (R Alphabet)

6. GAIUS JULIUS CAESAR (X Alphabet)

7. BROUGHT THE LATIN LANGUAGE HERE (Z Alphabet)

8. IN FIFTY FIVE B.C. (A Alphabet)

___Messages to Decipher___

9. What creature hops about and explodes near a naked flame?
MX MW E KEWLSTTIV (E Alphabet)

10. What creature says 'baa' and fights at sea?
ZNOY OY G'HGZZRKYNKKV¦(G Alphabet)

11. What creature bleats, has toggles and also a hood?
VG VF N QHSSRY TBNG (N Alphabet)

12. What creature feeds on millet and is often found in jams?
PDEO EO W XQZCANEYWN (W Alphabet)

WHICH ANIMAL RUNS VERY FAST
AND KEEPS YOU WARM ?

13. AL AK S OAFVUZWWLSZ (S Alphabet)

BORROWING FOREIGN LETTERS

These ciphers look much more difficult than they really are because they make use of unfamiliar foreign alphabets. One of them uses the Cyrillic alphabet which is named after Cyril (827 – 869AD), who was a Christian missionary to the Slav peoples. This alphabet is used nowadays for Russian and other Slavonic languages. The second alphabet shown below is that used in modern Greek. The letters used for the ciphers are a mixture of capitals and ordinary letters. No knowledge of either language is needed to decipher these messages, but it does need great care to correctly identify the unfamiliar shapes of the letters.

Cyrillic Letters

A	B	C	D	E	F	G	H	I	J	K	L	M	N	O	P	Q	R	S	T	U	V	W	X	Y	Z
Ф	Д	Б	э	Я	ф	Г	ж	И	ы	П	щ	Ю	Ъ	Щ	Й	Л	ю	Ц	и	Э	д	б	Ж	я	З

Greek Letters

A	B	C	D	E	F	G	H	I	J	K	L	M	N	O	P	Q	R	S	T	U	V	W	X	Y	Z
ω	γ	ψ	χ	δ	φ	υ	τ	ε	Ω	ν	α	ς	ζ	η	λ	ι	β	μ	σ	χ	θ	ξ	ο	π	ρ

Examples

A

plaintext ➡ FATHER AND SON

cryptogram ➡ фФижЯю ФЪэ ЦЩЪ

B

plaintext ➡ MOTHER AND DAUGHTER

cryptogram ➡ ςηστδβ ωζχ χωχυτσδβ

30

Messages to Decipher

1. бжИБж ЪЯбЦИФЯЯю эЩ ЦбИЪэщЯюЦ юЯФэ

Doctor, doctor I keep thinking I'm a bar of Kit Kat.

2. ижЯя юЯФэ ижЯ ФИЪФЪБИФщ Бюиюяц

3. бжИБж ЪЯбЦИФЯЯю эЩ юЯФэЦЯ БЩащЯБиЩюЦ юЯФэ

5. ξτωσ πηχ ζδδχ εμ ω γβδων

Doctor, doctor I keep thinking I'm a clock.

6. σβπ ζησ ση υδσ ση πηχζχ χλ

Doctor, doctor I keep thinking I'm a bus.

4. ижЯя юЯФэ ижЯ ДИЪэЯЯЯЯЪэЯъи

7. πηχ ζχμσ λχσ ω μσηλ ση στωσ ζηξ

"DOCTOR, DOCTOR I FEEL AS TENSE AS A VIOLIN STRING!

8. ψαδωβαπ πηχ ωβδ ωμ φεσ ωμ ω φεχχαδ

TWO-WAY CIPHERS

This cipher is an ingenious variation on Caesar's alphabets because it uses two alternative cipher alphabets in a systematic way. One is written in the normal direction and is indicated by a + sign and one is written in reverse and is indicated by a – sign. The card instrument, the TWO-WAY SLIDE is a convenient way of enciphering and deciphering this type of cipher.

Both the sender and the recipient have to know a simple code. This consists of two parts, a letter of the alphabet and a pattern of + and – signs. The letter indicates which cipher alphabet is to be used and the pattern of + and – signs determines which scale is used to encipher each letter. Repeat the pattern of + and – signs over all the letters of the plaintext. If the sign over a letter is a +, use the upper scale to encipher it. If it is a -, use the lower scale. Deciphering two-way cryptograms proceeds in the same manner, but of course reading from the cipher letter to the plaintext letter.

_____Examples_____

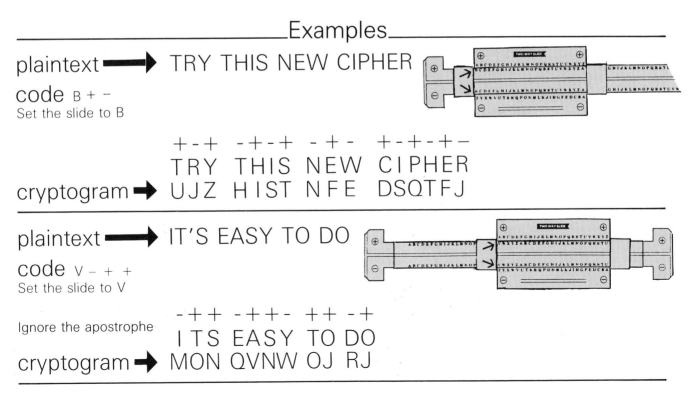

plaintext ➡ TRY THIS NEW CIPHER

code B + –
Set the slide to B

```
+-+  -+-+  - + -  +-+-+-
TRY  THIS  NEW    CIPHER
```
cryptogram ➡ UJZ HIST NFE DSQTFJ

plaintext ➡ IT'S EASY TO DO

code V – + +
Set the slide to V

Ignore the apostrophe

```
-++  -++-  ++  -+
ITS  EASY  TO  DO
```
cryptogram ➡ MON QVNW OJ RJ

A B C D E F G H I J K L M N O P Q R S T U V W X Y Z A B C D E F G H I J K L M N O P Q R S T U V W X Y Z

A B C D E F G H I J K L M N O P Q R S T U V W X Y Z A B C D E F G H I J K L M N O P Q R S T U V W X Y Z

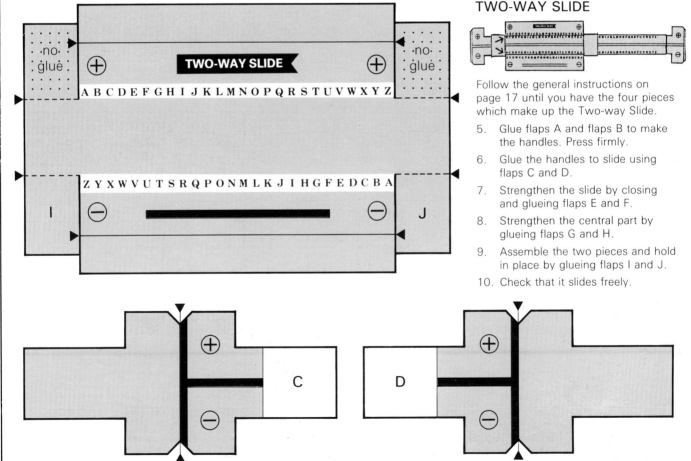

TWO-WAY SLIDE

Follow the general instructions on page 17 until you have the four pieces which make up the Two-way Slide.

5. Glue flaps A and flaps B to make the handles. Press firmly.

6. Glue the handles to slide using flaps C and D.

7. Strengthen the slide by closing and glueing flaps E and F.

8. Strengthen the central part by glueing flaps G and H.

9. Assemble the two pieces and hold in place by glueing flaps I and J.

10. Check that it slides freely.

TWO-WAY SLIDE

A B C D E F G H I J K L M N O P Q R S T U V W X Y Z

no glue · no glue

Z Y X W V U T S R Q P O N M L K J I H G F E D C B A

I   J

C   D

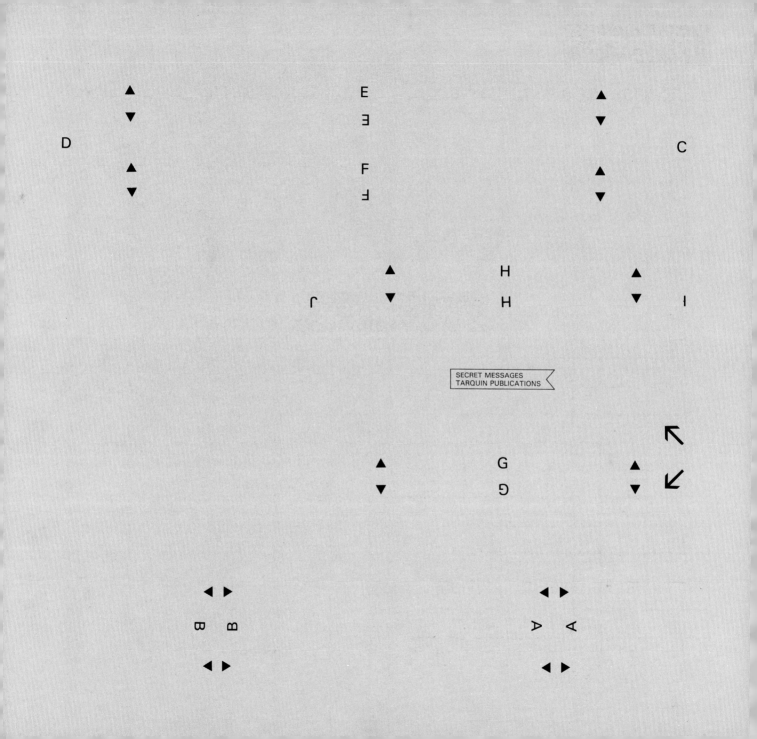

SECRET MESSAGES
TARQUIN PUBLICATIONS

___Messages to Encipher___

1. ONE SWALLOW DOESN'T MAKE A
   SUMMER
   (B + −)

2. A BIRD IN THE HAND IS WORTH TWO IN
   THE BUSH
   (M + − −)

3. BIRDS OF A FEATHER FLOCK TOGETHER
   (S − + −)

___Messages to Decipher___

4. Which lager do birds drink?
   KYSADJFL TGSPC GSQWG (S + −)

5. Where do parrots study?
   CW WVH SOOBJHFVQLA (D − + +)

6. How do hawks carry their shopping?
   DESV PXBB DL CPS EWOFFSO VXQP (X − +)

CROSSWORD

7. Find the bird to complete the crossword

   a) URAQCKM (C + −)

   b) SEQTEWB (F − − +)

   c) MXUFYEGTER (J − + −)

   d) YUMIIQCA (Q − +)

   e) LTFWFSKMKG (T + + −)

   f) INNFXPGBINX (C + − +)

   g) ?????? ??????

With a codeword and a simple grid it is possible to create cipher alphabets where letters are mixed in an apparently random fashion. The codeword can be a single word, but it can also be a phrase with its spaces and punctuation removed. The codeword is entered into the grid, ignoring any letters which are repeated in the codeword. Then the unused letters of the alphabet are entered, in order, into the remaining spaces of the grid, working horizontally. The cipher alphabet is then obtained from the columns of the grid.

_____Example_____

A plaintext ➡ SECRET MESSAGES

codeword ➡ BAD BOY

B	A	D	O	Y
C	E	F	G	H
I	J	K	L	M
N	P	Q	R	S
T	U	V	W	X
Z				

codeword grid ➡

cipher alphabet

A	B	C	D	E	F	G	H	I	J	K	L	M	N	O	P	Q	R	S	T	U	V	W	X	Y	Z
B	C	I	N	T	Z	A	E	J	P	U	D	F	K	Q	V	O	G	L	R	W	Y	H	M	S	X

cryptogram ➡ LTIGTR FTLLBATL

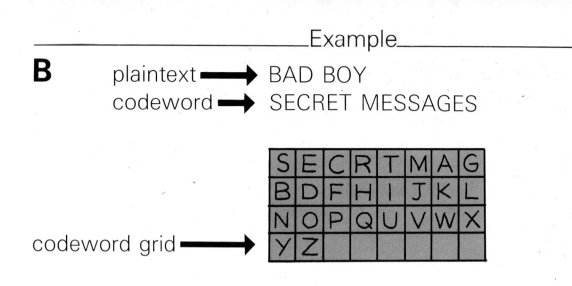

B   plaintext ➡ BAD BOY
      codeword ➡ SECRET MESSAGES

S	E	C	R	T	M	A	G
B	D	F	H	I	J	K	L
N	O	P	Q	U	V	W	X
Y	Z						

codeword grid ➡

cipher alphabet

A	B	C	D	E	F	G	H	I	J	K	L	M	N	O	P	Q	R	S	T	U	V	W	X	Y	Z
S	B	N	Y	E	D	O	Z	C	F	P	R	H	Q	T	I	U	M	J	V	A	K	W	G	L	X

cryptogram ➡ BSY BTL

_____

PUZZLES

___Messages to Encipher___   ___Messages to Decipher___

1. NEVER EAT SHREDDED WHEAT
   (codeword MOTHER)

2. EVERY GOOD BOY DESERVES FAVOURS
   (codeword FATHER)

3. RICHARD OF YORK GAVE BATTLE IN VAIN
   (codeword SISTER)

4. Which fish moves on wheels?
   TI TC IMY VOFFYV CDHIY
   (codeword HADDOCK)

5. Which dog is always on the phone?
   WEO YRPKOZ MOFOBDOM RU FRIMQO
   (codeword TERRIER)

KEYWORD CIPHERS

Any message written in a single cipher alphabet is fairly easy to decipher by even an amateur cryptanalyst if it is reasonably long. In English certain letters are much more frequently used than others and it is not difficult to identify the cipher letters for E and T. Then it is possible to find H and A and so on. The longer the message, the easier this becomes. If the message is written in some other language and then is enciphered it is even possible to find out which language it is by counting the frequency of each letter in the ciphertext.

The natural response by cryptographers to this problem is to mix several different cipher alphabets in the same message. The keyword then indicates which cipher alphabet to use to encipher each plaintext letter. The example below uses four different Caesar's alphabets in turn. This is quite sufficient to upset any simple analysis of letter frequency.

Such ciphers are best enciphered and deciphered using the VIGENERE SLIDE or the ALPHABET DISC, dealing with all the letters in each alphabet in turn.

_____Example_____

plaintext ➡ NO PARKING
keyword ➡ CARS

CA RSCARSC
NO PARKING

cryptogram ➡ PO GSTKZFI

using alphabet disc

C alphabet   A alphabet   R alphabet   S alphabet

PUZZLES

___Messages to Encipher___

1. A CIPHER DISC
   (keyword BIRDS)

2. GOES ROUND AND ROUND
   (keyword BEES)

3. THE LETTERS EVER CHANGING
   (keyword FISHES)

4. IT HELPS ME IN CRYPTOGRAPHY
   (keyword SNAKES)

5. BY ALPHABETS ARRANGING
   (keyword LIZARDS)

___Messages to Decipher___

6. Which dance do vampires like best?
   ZHV QIPMDRYOQ UF TZCTYE
   (keyword GARLIC)

7. Where does Dracula keep his savings?
   JN MZF BEGPD USOK
   (keyword BATS)

8. What sort of boat does Dracula cruise on?
   S QZCYV KSGCWA CT MGJFGO
   (keyword SPOOK)

9. Why does Dracula have no friends?
   CPQOXTP VS GSTJSV QPCDOF MOHWZ
   (keyword BLOOD)

WHAT SORT OF PASTA DO GHOSTS LIKE?

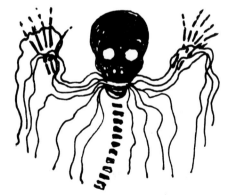

10. MVEB DHJE WG XOT VHHCKJZXHTL (keyword TOADS)

41

CODEWORDS and KEYNUMBERS

This cipher uses a codeword, but not directly as in some of the earlier ciphers. It is used to create a keynumber which in turn is used to generate a cipher alphabet. The letters of the codeword have to be numbered in alphabetical order. In the case of PARIS A = 1, I = 2, P = 3, R = 4, S = 5. Then the letters of the codeword in their original order give the keynumber. Use this keynumber to label the columns of a rectangular grid. Then enter a normal alphabet into the grid and use the columns in the keynumber order to make the cipher alphabet. It is then a simple process to encipher or decipher the message.

It would be easy to believe that a method like this would produce a cipher which is hard to break. It does produce a well mixed cipher alphabet, but we must remember that if any single cipher alphabet is used for a long message, then it can be broken quite easily by the method of letter frequency. The response is to change the codeword every few lines. Each change produces a new cipher alphabet and upsets any count of the letter frequency. PARIS, LONDON, ROME, BERLIN, would give four different cipher alphabets which could be used in turn and so confuse any attempt at cryptanalysis.

_____Example_____

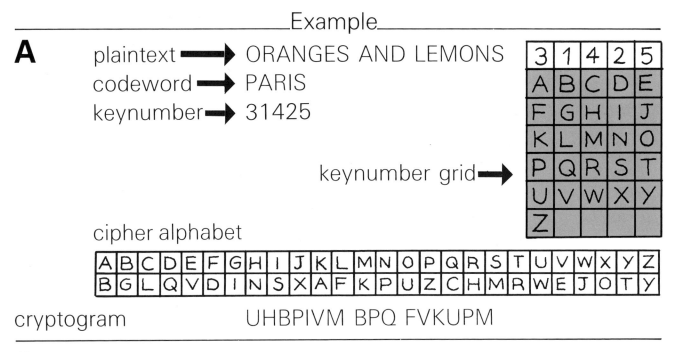

A

plaintext ➡ ORANGES AND LEMONS

codeword ➡ PARIS

keynumber ➡ 31425

keynumber grid ➡

3	1	4	2	5
A	B	C	D	E
F	G	H	I	J
K	L	M	N	O
P	Q	R	S	T
U	V	W	X	Y
Z				

cipher alphabet

A	B	C	D	E	F	G	H	I	J	K	L	M	N	O	P	Q	R	S	T	U	V	W	X	Y	Z
B	G	L	Q	V	D	I	N	S	X	A	F	K	P	U	Z	C	H	M	R	W	E	J	O	T	Y

cryptogram   UHBPIVM BPQ FVKUPM

B

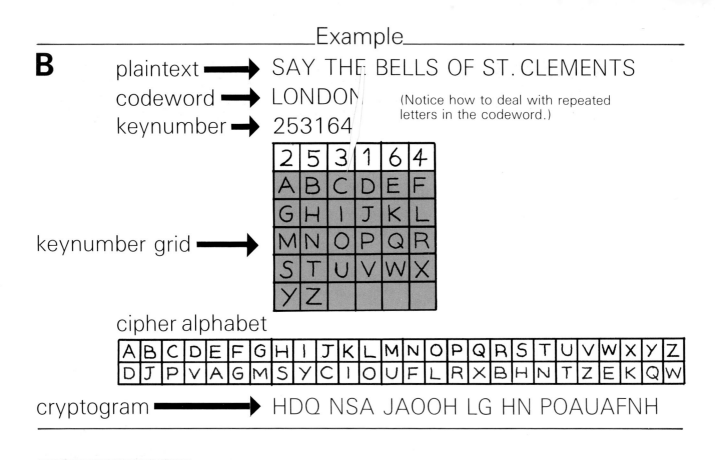

plaintext ➡ SAY THE BELLS OF ST. CLEMENTS

codeword ➡ LONDON

(Notice how to deal with repeated letters in the codeword.)

keynumber ➡ 253164

2	5	3	1	6	4
A	B	C	D	E	F
G	H	I	J	K	L
M	N	O	P	Q	R
S	T	U	V	W	X
Y	Z				

keynumber grid ➡

cipher alphabet

A	B	C	D	E	F	G	H	I	J	K	L	M	N	O	P	Q	R	S	T	U	V	W	X	Y	Z
D	J	P	V	A	G	M	S	Y	C	I	O	U	F	L	R	X	B	H	N	T	Z	E	K	Q	W

cryptogram ➡ HDQ NSA JAOOH LG HN POAUAFNH

PUPLES PUZZLES

_____Messages to Encipher_____

1. MIDNIGHT IN MOSCOW
   (codeword ROME)

2. MOONLIGHT IN VERMONT
   (codeword BERLIN)

3. SPRINGTIME IN PARIS
   (codeword LISBON)

_____Messages to Decipher_____

4. NECB OIO BES SAA XCV BH BES NEIXQ
   (codeword OSLO)

5. D RDZF DG D PGME EXFG DA IFCNFG
   (codeword PRAGUE)

6. HPAR HYAFL LPKYL GXR PAL EK DYYR
   (codeword ATHENS)

7. QUC PFACZCDQ JI RJWEKC
   (codeword VIENNA)

SUGGESTIONS

The ciphers in this book are just a few of all the ciphers that have been invented over many years in the ingenious battle of wits between cryptographers and cryptanalysts. It is very interesting to try to invent new ciphers of your own and then test them to see how good they are. A cipher is a good one if it is easy to encipher and decipher messages with the key, but very difficult for anyone else to discover. Here are five suggestions using transposition ideas and five suggestions using substitution ideas.

Transposition ideas

1. Why not try reversing the letters of the cryptogram after the cryptogram has been made.

SEC RETM ESSA GES
becomes
SEG ASSE MTER CES

2. Or reverse the letters in each group.

SEC RETM ESSA GES
becomes
CES MTER ASSE SEG

3. Try moving letter groups around using a keynumber. Keynumber 2431 gives the cryptogram.

1   2   3   4
SEC RETM ESSA GES
keynumber 2431 gives
RETM GES ESSA SEC

4. Use the nulls in various agreed places to help make up complete rectangles. Letter groups of 4, 5 or 6 look most like real words.

S	E	C	R
E	T	M	E
S	S	A	G
E	S	Z	Z

S	E	C
R	E	T
M	E	S
S	A	G
E	S	Q

5. Design your own grille, and possibly write the words down the spaces rather than across. Use several marks to show that the grille can be used in several different positions.

S		R		E		A		E
E			E	M		S	G	
C		T			S		•S	

1.

Any set of 26 signs can be used to replace the letters of the alphabet. Why not use musical notes?

A B C D E F G H I   J K L M N O P Q R   S T U V W X Y Z

2.

Develop the Polybius Square idea into a 3 x 9 rectangle and then use decimals or fractions. Try other shaped rectangles or use a square with the digits 67890 instead of 12345.

	1	2	3	4	5	6	7	8	9
1	A	B	C	D	E	F	G	H	I
2	J	K	L	M	N	O	P	Q	R
3	S	T	U	V	W	X	Y	Z	

3·1 1·5 1·3 2·9 1·5 3·2

¾ ⅕ ¾ ¾ ⅟ ⅟ ⅕ ¾

3.

If you use a codeword to make a cipher, choose one which is easy to remember such as the names of friends or family.

SUSA NS US ANSUS ANSUS

MEET ME IN SAINT LOUIS

4.

Make a new alphabet disc with the cipher letters in random order or replaced with symbols or letters belonging to foreign alphabets.

5.

Have fun with friends giving each other code names, code numbers or signs that only you and they know. Keep them simple so that they are easy to remember.

OO7   ● ━   KING KONG

5. RANDOM BREAK CIPHERS

1, 2 and 3 are correct so long as all the letters are there in their original order but the words are broken up in a different way.
4. WHY WAS THE CRAB SENT TO PRISON
5. BECAUSE HE KEPT PINCHING THINGS
6. WHICH TOOTHPASTE DO SHARKS USE
7. THEY USE AQUAFLESH OF COURSE
8. WHY DID THE FISH BLUSH
9. BECAUSE IT SAW THE OCEAN'S BOTTOM

7. ZIGZAG CIPHERS

1. IEAATEEKN.RLXTHWEED
2. TCEETE.HSIHRSAYOS.IPISU
3A. WEJYITNNTMSC.ENOLSEIGOUI
3B. WJINTS.ENOLSEIGOUI.EYTNMC
4. WRITE YOUR LETTERS CLEARLY
5. MAKE THE SPACES BIG
6. WORK STEADILY AND CAREFULLY
7. DON'T ZAG WHEN YOU SHOULD ZIG
8. ONE HUNTS FLEAS AND THE OTHER FLEES HUNTS

9. SQUARE CIPHERS

1. MER AAI KGD
2. PNTO UAHR TLED ILWS
3. WEOFH RALRE ICUOT THMMO ECNTP
4. HSERS EOWES RUSTA EREMG INCEE
5. ONE MINUTE
6. FOUR HOURS
7. SEVEN DAYS IN A WEEK
8. FIFTY TWO WEEKS MAKE EACH YEAR
9. ONE BOARDS PLANES THE SECOND PLANES BOARDS

11. RECTANGLE CIPHERS

1. IBO AIU MGB ITL NRE
2. GKM OLE QYR UTI IOC CAA
3. GAES EFDP TOPO MRAR EGST
4. HTOKE EIDIR RSLNI EGUAC IOCMA
5. JACK BE NIMBLE
6. PEASE PUDDING HOT
7. BAA BAA BLACK SHEEP
8. ONE TWO BUCKLE MY SHOE

9. SIMPLE SIMON MET A PIEMAN
10. a) MADAGASCAR b) GREENLAND c) AUSTRALIA d) SRILANKA e) MAURITIUS f) NEW GUINEA g) GREAT BRITAIN

13. RECTANGLES and NULLS

1. TPA ETP AHE RER UPQ
2. UEIP SSAH EPLE TECR HCIQ
3. RHTAL EITRL ASEEY DLRFQ TECUQ
4. PNEEK ATSQL SHSUY SEAIQ OMGCQ
5. KHIMNE EENAST ENFTEQ PEOICQ TWRORQ
6. DSRBERO OTEEIUN YIMRNCS OLETSTQ ULMHTIQ
7. IT WAS HERCULE BIRO (ZYXW)
8. IT IS BRITISH AERO SPACE OF COURSE (YZ)
9. THEY HAVE TO TRAVEL BY OMNIBUZZES (YZ)
10. IT IS CALLED A DO-YOU-THINK-HE-SAURUS (X)
11. IT IS CALLED A COLA BEAR (X)

15. RECTANGLES and KEYNUMBERS

1. LGOZ INDS WELN SOIZ LDCZ
2. CCOPBZ EASSIZ KTSASZ ANANSE MOTOOL
3. AROOTEZ ETVTIXS POEHEPZ WNANRES LTLENRZ
4. ONE CHECKS EYES AND ONE EYES CHEQUES
5. ONE GROUP SELLS SHARES THE OTHER SHARES CELLS (XX)
6. a) MANCHESTER b) GLOUCESTER c) ABERDEEN d) STIRLING e) EDINBURGH f)COLCHESTER f) PETERBOROUGH

19. GRILLE CIPHERS

1A. USE MY NEW VIDEO CAMERA
1B. CHECK YOUR DATA PLEASE
2A. PUT THE PLAINTEXT HERE
2B. HE MUST GO TO AUSTRALIA

21. OPEN LETTER CIPHERS

1. FIND The key
2. READ THe notes
3. Book A Taxi For The Station

23. PIG PEN CIPHER

1. ⸮⸮⸮⸮ ⸮⸮⸮⸮⸮ ⸮⸮ ⸮⸮⸮ ⸮⸮⸮ ⸮⸮⸮
2. ⸮⸮ ⸮⸮⸮⸮⸮ ⸮⸮⸮ ⸮⸮⸮⸮⸮ ⸮⸮⸮⸮
3. ⸮⸮⸮⸮⸮⸮ ⸮⸮⸮ ⸮⸮⸮⸮⸮⸮⸮ ⸮⸮⸮⸮⸮⸮⸮
4. ⸮⸮ ⸮⸮⸮⸮⸮⸮ ⸮⸮⸮ ⸮⸮⸮ ⸮⸮⸮⸮
5. CREAM EGGS OF COURSE
6. A POLICE INSPECTRE
7. A SOUR PUSS
8. YOU WILL GET THE COLLIE WOBBLES

25. POLYBIUS SQUARE

1. 44.23.15. 11.33.13.24.15.33.44. 22.42.15.15.25. 52.42.24.44.15.42. 35.34.31.54.12.24.45.43.
2. 52.42.34.44.15. 52.34.42.14.43. 24.33. 52.11.54.43. 52.23.24.13.23. 52.15.42.15. 14.15.51.24.34.45.43.
3. USING NUMBERS FOR LETTERS
4. GREAT PUZZLES HE SET US
5. IN A CIPHER MORE SECRET THAN PREVIOUS
6. a) SWEDEN b) PORTUGAL c) GREECE d) NETHERLANDS e) DENMARK f) SWITZERLAND

29. CAESAR'S ALPHABETS

1. PEXMR MW E PERKYEKI
2. HZ KLHK HZ KLHK JHU IL
3. UF WUXXQP FTQ YUSTFK DAYMZE
4. QDT DEM YJI AYBBYDW CU
5. ZKJ R GZKP KYRK FCU XVVQVI
6. DXFRP GRIFRP ZXBPXO
7. AQNTFGS SGD KZSHM KZMFTZFD GDQD
8. IN FIFTY FIVE B.C.
9. IT IS A GASHOPPER
10. THIS IS A BATTLESHEEP
11. IT IS A DUFFEL GOAT
12. THIS IS A BUDGERICAR
13. IT IS A WIND CHEETAH

31. BORROWING FOREIGN LETTERS

1. WHICH NEWSPAPER DO SWINDLERS READ
2. THEY READ THE FINANCIAL CRIMES
3. WHICH NEWSPAPER DO REFUSE COLLECTORS READ
4. THEY READ THE BINDEPENDENT

5. WHAT YOU NEED IS A BREAK
6. TRY NOT TO GET TOO WOUND UP
7. YOU MUST PUT A STOP TO THAT NOW
8. CLEARLY YOU ARE AS FIT AS A FIDDLE

35. TWO-WAY CIPHERS

1. PNF IXAMPPE EMFIOH NALW B IVONWS
2. M KDDI DZ SEQ ELZI DE PXDSE FPX UY STH KGTE
3. QAAOK DM S MNSYKWA MDDPC YDYNYZNA
4. STARLING BLACK LABEL
5. AT THE POLYTECHNIC
6. THEY HAVE TO USE HARRIER BAGS
7. a) SKYLARK b) MALLARD c) WOODPECKER d) REDSHANK e) SANDMARTIN f) GOLDEN EAGLE g) YELLOW HAMMER

37. CODEWORD ALPHABETS

1. UYWYV YMF EJVYQQYQ RJYMF
2. YWYVP CHHQ BHP QYEYVWYE AFWHOVE
3. DHGBSDM OZ QODV ISRU ASPPTU HJ RSHJ
4. IT IS THE ROLLER SKATE
5. THE GOLDEN RECEIVER OF COURSE

41. KEYWORD CIPHERS

1. B KZSZFZ ULKD
2. HSIK SSYFE ERV SSYFE
3. YPW SILYMJZ INJZ UOEFLQFN
4. AG HOPHK ZE SR UJLPDSYJNPRC
5. MG ZLGKSMMSS RUJLVFIEJ
6. THE FANGDANGO OF COURSE
7. IN THE BLOOD BANK
8. A BLOOD VESSEL OF COURSE
9. BECAUSE HE DRIVES PEOPLE BATTY
10. THEY LOVE TO EAT SPOOKGHETTI

43. CODEWORDS and KEYNUMBERS

1. BKPFKCGA KF BJZLJM
2. QDDWKTHNL TW XYVQDWL
3. ELXZYNKZSB ZY LDXZE
4. WHAT DID THE EGG SAY TO THE WHISK
5. I GIVE IN I KNOW WHEN I'M BEATEN
6. WHAT WEARS SHOES BUT HAS NO FEET
7. THE PAVEMENT OF COURSE

SEMAPHORE

Semaphore is a code which was used by sailors to send messages from ship to ship before the days of radio.

Don't miss the secret message in the semaphore code along the tops of the pages.